When the People Speak:

Selected Words on Life in the African American Experience

By

Dr. Benjamin Foster, Jr.

Published by

L & F Associates

P. O. Box 1724

Hartford, CT. 06144

© Copyright 2013 by Benjamin Foster, Jr.

Fourth Printing

October 2016

DEDICATION

To the Creator of us all;

To the memory of my mother, Miriam Ferrell-Foster, my first teacher; she encouraged me to love learning.

To the memory of my maternal grandmother, Rosa Ferrell; Each Sunday after church we would sit in the swing on the front porch while "Grandie" read the comic strips to me and my younger siblings, until I could read. Her stories about the Ferrell-Turner families during and after enslavement as told to her by her grandmother, helped developed my historical frame of reference and appreciation for the written word and oratory. To all the educators who have assisted me on my intellectual journey, especially those women and men in the racially segregated public schools of Raleigh, North Carolina.

To Mrs. Nancy Wogan; a loving Quaker and writer;

To my family and the children yet unborn; May the almighty make their way easy.

To my beloved sons; Benjamin Bayete and Suliman Samuel may this humble effort enhance your knowledge and be a continuous well of refreshing cool water.

To the grandchildren: Solé Amee and Damien Jafar.

ACKNOWLEDGEMENTS

My immense appreciation to Joycelyn Jackman; her word-processing and dedication to the task was invaluable.

A very special expression of gratitude is given to my wife, Professor Walton Brown-Foster, for her copious technical assistance and kind heart.

Contents

Preface

Dear Reader,

I am observing the brilliant New England foliage as the grey squirrels scamper for nuts, while experiencing ballads rendered by Gene Ammons and John Coltrane. I search for words to convey my thoughts as I mellow in the rays of life's double sunset. Words, spoken and printed have always motivated me to ponder the essence of being-ness. It is no wonder then that I believe that the African American experience in these United States is of epic proportion. It remains the greatest untold story in the annals of modern history. The words and thoughts of African Americans have inspired and fed the very sinews of America's soul, if the truth be told. Whether it was in the plantation kitchen, slave cabins, cotton fields, low country rice patties, song lyrics, sermons, or literature, African American philosophy and soul-force has been encapsulated by the dominant culture. Having caught the "A-train," it is now Americana.

I have compiled these "words –on-life" to share with you, because they tell the story and capture the essence of the ongoing journey and struggle of African Americans from a multidimensional perspective. But more importantly, I have striven to provide the young with historical perspectives in this critical period. That is to say, for the first time in the African American sojourn their physical labor is no longer vital to the

American economy. The high unemployment rate among African American males has been epidemic in urban inner-cities for nearly fifty years. I have striven to share words of inspiration in this increasingly violent and perplexing environment our children and youth have inherited. We are daily bombarded with stories of their murder and mayhem by the printed and electronic media. Now an urban people, the African American community is reeling from its greatest challenge since the end of enslavement: homicide, suicide, family dissolution, persistent male unemployment, and incarceration.

Finally, the "folk sayings" street language, or colloquialisms are added spicing.

Keep the Faith,

Benjamin Foster, Jr.

CONTEXT

Benjamin Banneker
Astronomer/Mathematician

Excerpts from Letter to Thomas Jefferson

Sir, I freely and cheerfully acknowledge, that I am of the African American race, and in that color which is natural to them of the deepest dye; and it is under a sense of the most profound gratitude to the Supreme Ruler of the Universe.... suffer me to recall your mind to that time, in which the arms and tyranny of the British crown were exerted, this, sir, was a time when you clearly saw into the injustice of slavery.... here was a time, in which your tender feelings for yourselves had engaged you with the proper ideas of the great violation of liberty, but, sir how pitiable is it to reflect, that although you were so fully convinced of the benevolence of the Father of Mankind, and of his equal and impartial distribution of these rights and privileges....that you should at the same time counteract his mercies, in detaining by fraud and violence so numerous a part of my brethren under groaning captivity......

HISTORY

John Hope Franklin, Ph.D.
(Historian)

If the house is to be set in order, one cannot begin with the present; we must begin with the past.

John Henrik Clark
(Historian)

"History is a clock that tells a people their historical time of day. It is a compass that people use to locate themselves on the map of human geography. A people's history tells a people where they have been and what they still must be and where they still must go."

Carter G. Woodson, Ph. D.
(Historian)

If a race has no history, if it has no worthwhile traditions, it becomes a negligible factor in the thought of the world and stands in danger of being exterminated.

Justice Roger Brook Taney
(Supreme Court Justice in Plessey v Ferguson)

...no African, whether slave or free could claim U. S. Citizenship.... or had no rights which any white man was bound to respect....

Bayard Rustin
(Civil Rights Activist)

The murder of Dr. King tells Negroes that if one of the greatest among them is not safe from the assassin's bullet, then what can the least of them hope for?

Na'im Akbar, Ph.D.
(Psychologist)

...The experience of slavery in this country was like no other experience in the history of modern man...

We need to understand that slavery presented some serious problems. We are still dealing with some of those problems. Any kind of trauma (psychic trauma, social trauma, cultural trauma) plagues people for generations to come.

John Hope Franklin, Ph.D.
(Historian)

"All too frequently….history overlook the role of African
Americans in the exploration and settlement of the
American West….black Americans, slave and free, were
involved in the process….their reliability and integrity
have often suffered at the hands of many recognized
historians….their presence and indeed their contribution
can hardly be denied"….

…Looking back on almost four centuries…in the Western
world, African Americans could correctly visualize
themselves, from the beginning, as an integral part of the
struggle for freedom…frequently, they were active
participants in the valiant warfare to destroy bigotry,
repression, and subjugation. They had become an integral
part of Western culture and civilization, and their fate
was inextricably, connected with it. The rejection that
they had suffered doubtlessly wounded them
considerably, but such treatment also gave them a
perspective and an objectivity that others had greater
difficulty in achieving….they could…point out more
clearly than some…the weakness that seemed to be
inherent in Western civilization.

Dr. Martin L. King, Jr.
(Theologian)

History does not pose problems without eventually producing solutions. The disenchanted, the disadvantaged, and disinherited seem at times of deep crisis to summon up some sort of genius that enables them to perceive and capture the appropriate weapons to carve out their destiny.

Robert Staples, Ph. D.
(Sociologist)

Slavery had its greatest impact on the family life of the Africans brought to the United States. Most of the slaves who came in the beginning were males. The black female population was not equal to the number of males until 1840.

The system of slavery eliminated any protection that black women had against male sexual advances…black females… were sexually used to maintain the chastity of white females.

Lerone Bennett, Jr.
(Author of Before the Mayflower)

...in the 1970's, Black Americans came to one of the fundamental turning points in Black life. In the decade of the sixties, Blacks had made unprecedented gains in education, income and politics. Here for almost the first time in American history, was real movement towards concrete freedom and positive proof that America could overcome...racism. If that movement had continued and if it had been supported by the American government and corporate leaders, we would be living in a different world today.

Harry Belafonte
(Civil Rights Activist/Performing Artist)

The last thing Dr. King ever said to me in my home just before he went down to Memphis. He said "You know, we fought long and hard for integration, as we should have. And I know we're going to get it. That's a fait accompli. But I tell you, Harry, I've come to the realization that really deeply troubles me. I've come to the realization that I think we maybe integrating into a burning house".

Charlie Parker went with me many a night to Brooklyn and to Harlem and to places just to play before DuBois spoke and before Robeson spoke. And once he did it, he began to say "Hey, Harry man, you get more of those gigs, call me". No cash flow at all!

…we are in the greatest jeopardy we have ever been in….I think black culture as it sits in America, and as it sits in other places in the diaspora is under the greatest onslaught of negativity that has ever existed because of what monopoly capital is doing to control all the forces that buy and sell it…

Congressman George H. White
(Last Congressman to Serve in Post Reconstruction Era)

"This, Mr. Chairman, is perhaps the Negroes' temporary farewell to the American Congress; but let me say, Phoenix-like, he will rise up some day and come again. These parting words are in behalf of an outraged, heartbroken, bruised and bleeding, but God-fearing people, faithful, industrious, loyal, rising, people-full of fierce potential".

Dr. WEB Du Bois
(Author, Historian, and Co-founder N.A.A.C.P)

The Negro was freed as a penniless, landless, naked, ignorant laborer…instead of being led by others…they are gaining their own leaders, their own voices, their own ideas. Self-realization is coming slowly but surely to another of the world's great races, and Negroes are today girding themselves to fight in the van of progress not simply for their own rights as men, but for the ideals of the greater world in which they live, the emancipation of women, universal peace, democratic government….and human brotherhood…

…the more commercial a proposition slavery became the more drastic were the laws enacted against education, which might make the Negro discontented or restless with his lot…

…all Art is propaganda and ever must be, despite the wailing of the purists. I stand in utter blamelessness and say that whatever art I have for writing has been used always for propaganda for gaining the rights of black folk to love and enjoy…do care when propaganda is confined to one side while the other is stripped and silenced.

…the problem of the 20th century is the color line…

Just as a tree without roots is dead, a people without history or cultural roots also becomes a dead people.

Justice Thurgood Marshall
(First Black Supreme Court Justice)

…"as I look around, I see not a nation of unity but of division --- Afro and white, indigenous and immigrant, rich and poor educated and illiterate… But there is a price to be paid for division and isolation"

…the only way this Court can decide this case in opposition to our position…we submit…is to find that for some reason Negroes are inferior to all other human beings…it can't be color because there are Negroes as white as the drifted snow, with blue eyes, and they are just as segregated as the colored man. The only thing it can be is an inherent determination that the people who were formerly in slavery…shall be kept as near that stage as possible…we submit, that this court should make it clear that that is not what our constitution stands for…

Constance Baker Motley
(Federal Judge)

In this century, we have essentially repeated the gains and losses of the last century. The next century promises more of the same.

We African Americans have spent the major part of the 20th century battling racism.

EDUCATION

Constance Baker Motley
(Federal Judge)

In high school, I discovered myself. I was interested in race relations and the legal profession.

Alex Haley
(Author)

We will die without our young people.

Benjamin Foster, Jr., Ed.D.
(Author/Educator)

The educator must consider his/her intellectual development and cultural road map and/or context in which teaching occurs. It is the educator's duty to make lessons, relevant to his/her students. Teaching is truly an act of love.

Maya Angelou
(Educator/Poet)

Education helps one cease being in strange situations.

Dr. Benjamin E. Mays
(Educator/Theologian)

"Teachers and students should be more than good scholars; they should be good men and women".

"The beauty of an ideal lies in the fact that it is bound by neither nation nor race, restricted by neither class or caste."

"…341 years of disability made millions of Negroes believe that they were inferior-so much that millions of Negroes since 1865 accept without protest their inferior status, believed like an inferior…341 years of disability destroyed the ambition of millions, crushed the potential genius of thousands, and cut the nerves of aspirations of hundreds of thousands…"

"…the illiterate man who would overcome his ignorance must study as we protest and demonstrate for justice and equality…such is your plight and mine…for he who starts behind in the great race of life must forever remain behind or run faster than the man in front…"

…let us not become a race of employees, only looking for a soft bed somebody else has made up. But let us also become a race of employers, blazing new paths and building new enterprises…size alone is not the criterion of excellence…"

Janice E. Hale, Ph.D.
(Educator)

"There is a need to articulate a pedagogy that includes an environment drawn from African culture, teaching strategies, embedded in African – American learning styles, and materials relevant to the African-American experience…there should be an integration of African-American culture in all of its diversity throughout the curriculum…"

Benjamin Foster, Jr., Ed.D.
(Educator/Author)

…"in this advanced-technological society, our children must receive education to thrive, not merely survive."

William Julius Wilson, Ph. D.
(Sociologist)

We shouldn't rely solely on standardized tests because they don't really capture true potential.

You can't capture the importance of the environment unless you recognize the interaction between social conditions and cultural conditions.

Elijah Muhammad
(Leader, Nation of Islam)

I am for the acquiring of knowledge or the accumulating of knowledge. First, my people must be taught knowledge of self. The lack of knowledge of self is a prevailing condition among my people…we need education…which removes us from the shackles of slavery and servitude…"an education which will make our people produce jobs for self"…

Asa G. Hilliard
(Psychologist/Educator)

…Africa is the mother of the whole human family. Africa is also the mother of civilization. For thousands of years, African people were the premier teacher on the earth. A single nation in Africa, KMT (Egypt), demonstrated more than three thousand years unbroken civilization…a feat unmatched in human history…

…I am concerned because we seem to be riding in the caboose of a train, that is not headed for our

17

destination…African Americans seem to be trapped in the rhetoric…the parade of "problems" is endless as they flow from the fickle minds of public policy analyst…I am concerned because the problem with these "problems" is that they are not problems…but symptoms, because they are the predictable consequences of sustained, systematic, formal and informal, direct and indirect, overt and covert oppression and its legacy"

…"Many of our children are unable to decode the negative message about them in the media…many are unable to distinguish between and among the famous African American role models…treating fame as if it were our highest value…they see the fame but not the game"

…I would like to think our children would not be mere prisoners of mass common ideas. I want them to hear and to heed the call of destiny…

Carter G. Woodson
(Historian)

…"If you can control a man's thinking you do not have to worry about his actions. When you determine what a man shall think you do not have to concern yourself about what he will do. If you make a man feel he is inferior, you do not have to compel him to accept an inferior status, for he will seek it himself…"

…" A mind that remains in the present atmosphere never undergoes sufficient development to experience what is commonly known as thinking…the education of the Negro…becomes a perfect device for control from without…

Freeman A. Hrabowski, III Ph.D.
(Educator/Mathematician)

…Race did play a role. I've read a lot about Egyptology and the history of African Americans. I know it's important to instill those qualities in African American boys. They have to be aware of their culture and to know history in order to achieve. A lot of Black males don't know how rich a history of math and science we come from and how others have piggybacked on us. That's important for them to know, especially with all the negative things that are happening on the streets now…

James Baldwin
(Author)

"…If for example, one managed to change the curriculum in all the schools so that Negroes learned more about themselves and their real contributions to this culture, you would be liberating not only Negroes, you'd be liberating white people…if you are compelled to lie about one aspect of anybody's history, you must lie about it all…if you have to pretend that I hoed all that cotton because I loved you, then you have done something to yourself, you are mad."

Jonathan Kozol
(Author/Educator)

…I am startled to think how seldom any press reporter has observed the irony of naming segregated schools for Martin Luther King. Children reach the heart of these hypocrisies much quicker than the grown-ups and the experts do…

Nationwide, black children are three times as likely as white children to be placed in classes for the mentally retarded but only half as likely to be placed in classes for the gifted…"

…In the education catch-up game, we are entrapped by teaching to the tests…we are preparing a generation of robots. Kids are learning exclusively through rote…"

C. Eric Lincoln, Ph. D
(Author/Educator)

Black students...at the college and university level, resistance was more "reasoned," more restrained, and considerably more devious. In black studies, the university technique of giving black students what they think they want...black studies programs always seemed to have an "adjunctive" aura which stigmatized the students and professors associated with them...seldom did the host institution make a serious effort to fund, staff, or regulated them in a way that would level their institutional prestige...

"Black studies are a vital instrument in the determination of the quality of the future. It is not a discipline to be limited to black children...the white child should of course have the benefit of black studies at some level in his academic career...

Dr. Marva Collins
(Educator)

An error means a child needs help, not a reprimand or ridicule for doing something wrong.

Mary McLeod Bethune
(Founder of Bethune-Cookman College and National
Council of Negro Women)

For, I am my mother's daughter and the drums of Africa
still beat in my heart. They will not let me rest while
there is a single Negro boy or girl without a chance to
prove his worth.

Rudy Crew, Ed.D.
(Educator/Former Chancellor New York City and Miami
Schools)

In a world where a working toilet or sharp pencil is an
educational fantasy for many, many children, excuse my
lack of enthusiasm for pedagogical daydreaming…when
delivering quality education on a day to day basis to tens
of millions of Americans is so difficult a task, I think our
heads needs to come out of the clouds. This culture is not
going to fight off the darkness of ignorance when the
majority of us don't know how to use our minds as
weapons. I want results.

School systems that don't integrate day-to-day learning
with the needs of the economy, so kids learn to function
within the context of low, middle and high-end job
requirements for going into the surrounding
community's economic base…lose their leverage and

ultimately lose their way, leaving their community high and dry.

Caring, high expectations, and diverse approaches to learning are nothing but the timeless qualities of effective teaching, but their effectiveness in creating twenty first century people is limited by the nature of schools today. Nor are they distributed equitably and therefore efficiently.

If you want to teach, don't do it out of pity. Do it as you would any other profession, with the same focus and drive and determination...

Dr. Martin L. King, Jr.
(Theologian)

Education which stops with efficiency may prove the greatest menace to society...intelligence is not enough. Intelligence plus character — that is the goal of true education.

Miles Davis
(Jazz Musician)

When kids don't learn about their heritage in school, they just don't care about school. They turn to dope, to crack, because nobody cares about them. I know about this because I was into it when I was on drugs. I know that a lot of them drop into the underground culture because they   ain't gonna get no fairness from white people…

Na'im Akbar Ph.D.
(Educator/Psychologist)

…"the human being…is not restricted by instinct…the way that the human being is able to find out what he has to do, is by learning, by the development of consciousness, by beginning to study himself, study all the rest of creation, study his history as a human being, and in the process, discover the patterns which dignify and make him what he is…education is supposed to do this"…

John Oliver Killens
(Novelist)

A child must have a sense of selfhood, a knowledge that he is not here by sufferance that his forbears contributed to the country and to the world.

Malcolm X

Education is the passport to the future, for tomorrow belongs to those who prepare for it today.

W. Allison Davis
(Sociologist)

..."every black scholar should try to select a problem that contributed to racial advancement...the black scholar of whatever type has an integral role in the pattern of ongoing social change. Only history can judge how important a role it is, or will become"...

Dr. Vincent Harding
(Scholar/Activist)

"Systems do not exist apart from individuals. They are indeed, the creation and expression of men and women...in spite of the pain it often causes us, black scholars must not stop with systems when we identify the enemy"...

Samuel Edward Brown, Sr.
(Educator)

"Reading is one key to learning...I read."

BUSINESS/WEALTH

Chancellor Williams, Ph. D.
(Historian)

"Black political power can support, but never replace an organized economic power system within the race itself that gives it the resources to do what has to be done, the only move that will command the respect for Blacks as a people"…

Robert L. Johnson
(Entrepreneur & Founder of BET)

…Black unemployment remains double that of White Americans…in order to reverse these alarming trends, corporate America must view diversity as a business imperative, no less important than financial performance, succession planning, and share holder relations. The history of this country is replete with the positive things that can happen when you give minorities an opportunity. Unfortunately, it is also replete with hard facts that if minorities are denied an equal opportunity a gap in their socio-economic well-being will emerge, and that is exactly what is happening in the U.S. today and will continue to happen if a solution is not found.

George Washington Carver
(Scientist)

We have become ninety-nine percent money-mad. The method of living at home modestly and within our income, laying a little aside systematically for the proverbial rainy day which is due to come, can almost be listed among the lost arts.

Bessie Smith
(Blues Singer)

I've been rich and I've been poor, and rich is better.

Will Smith
(Actor)

Money and success don't change people; these merely amplify what is already there in their socio-economic well-being...that is exactly what is happening in the U.S. today and will continue to happen if a solution is not found.

Dr. Marvin Collins
(Educator)

Success doesn't come to you, you go to it.

Kareem Abdul-Jabbar
(Author/Hall of Fame Basketball Player)

I try to do the right thing at the right time. They may just
be little things, but usually they make the difference
between winning and losing.

David H. Swinton, Ph. D.
(Economist/President of Benedict College)

The 1980's will be recorded as a decade during which
progress towards racial equality in economic life for black
Americans as a group came to a grinding halt. The
Reagan and Bush administrations seemed to renounce
even the minimal Nixon gestures towards affirmative
action…the Reagan-Bush policy of neglect and
deregulation was based on their strong belief in the
virtues of market and self- help…

Earl Graves, Sr.
(Founder, Black Enterprise)

African Americans have made astounding progress in my life-time…according to a recent Nielsen study, black spending power is set to cross, the trillion-dollar threshold by 2015…many cite these and other realities of 21st century black America as ample evidence…we have finally overcome…But it's not true…roughly 25% of African Americans are still enmeshed in crushing poverty…leaving them behind to focus exclusively on building black wealth…is equivalent to shutting down the Underground Railroad and ending the abolitionist movement…

Claude Anderson, Ed. D.
(Educator/Entrepreneur)

Since wealth remains concentrated and rigidly locked in the hands of whites, black progress will be difficult. As far back as 1790, the richest 10 percent of white households held half of the nation's wealth. By the eve of the Civil War, one percent of wealthy whites owned 24 percent of the nation's wealth. One hundred years later, in 1969, they owned 24.9 percent…during the very same periods, black wealth remained between one and two percent. It is astounding that the percentage of wealth controlled by whites or blacks have not changed throughout the nation's involvement in the Civil War, emancipation of the slaves, Reconstruction, World War I, the Great Depression, World War II, Korean and Vietnam Wars, the Civil Rights movement…through it all, the wealthy white elite collectively held on to everything…

Gordon Parks, Sr.
(Award Winning Photographer, Film-Maker and Author)

The guy who takes a chance, who walks the line between the known and unknown, who is unafraid of failure will succeed.

John H. Johnson
(Entrepreneur/Philanthropist, Founder of Ebony Magazine)

Wealth is really what you own and control, not how much you have in your pockets.

Bill Russell
(Professional Basketball Player/Coach)

"…I had to work as hard to achieve my status in professional sports, as the president of General Motors"

Russell Simmons
(Entrepreneur)

The key ingredient to any kind of success is to never give less than your best.

Giving not trading or selling is the basis of success. There are no failures, only quitters.

Vernon Jordan
(Corporate Attorney)

Unless you're running scared all the time, you're gone.

Success is achieved and maintained by those who try and keep trying.

It takes 20 years to build a reputation and five minutes to ruin it. If you think about that, you'll do things differently.

If GM had kept up with technology like the computer
industry has, we would all be driving
$25 cars that got 1000 MPG.

William "Bill" Cosby
(Humorist and Educator)

In order to succeed, your desire for success should be
greater than your fear of failure.

Booker T. Washington
(Educator and Leader)

Success in business is founded upon attention to the small
things rather than large things.

Dr. George Washington Carver
(Scientist)

When you do the common things…in an uncommon way,
you will command the attention of the world.

Michael Jordan
(Athlete/Entrepreneur)

Success isn't something you chase. It is something you have to put forth the effort for constantly; then it'll come when you least expect it.

To be successful you have to be selfish, or else you never achieve. And once you get to your highest level, then you have to be unselfish. Stay in touch. Don't isolate.

Reginald Lewis
(Attorney/Entrepreneur)

Why should the white guys have all the fun?

I am very proud of the accomplishments of African Americans, but to dwell on race to see that as something that becomes part of my persona is a mistake, and I do everything I can to discourage it.

Steven Rogers
(Harvard Business School Senior Lecture on
Entrepreneurial Finance)

We have a wealth of black people who have technical and
financial backgrounds, so there is zero reason for there to
be no black people on boards today.

Bruce G. Gordon
(Board Member for CBS and Northrop Grumman)

When you are discussing diversity and trying to advance
particularly as it applies to supplier diversity or getting
people of color in senior roles – it's not just talking about
it to board colleagues; it's talking about it to management.

A. G. Gaston

(Businessman/Entrepreneur)

Money has no color.

Find a need and fill it. Successful businesses are
founded on the needs of people.

Money is no good unless it contributes something to the community, unless it builds a bridge to a better life.

INSPIRATION/UPLIFT

Mother Pollard
(Montgomery Bus Boycott Participant)

My feet is tired, but my soul is rested.

Stevie Wonder
(Composer/Musician)

Just because a man lacks the use of his eyes doesn't mean
he lacks vision.

Fannie Lou Hamer
(Civil Rights Activist/Icon)

When I liberate myself, I liberate others. If you don't
speak out ain't nobody going to speak out for you.

Maulana Karenga
(Educator/Activist)

To talk Black is to start talking "we" instead of "me"

Failure is not bad in itself, only resignation is bad.

He who convinces others appears to be together, but he
who convinces himself is together.

If by primitive you mean more natural, we need to be
more primitive.

Cannonball Adderly
(Jazz Musician)

Hip-ness is not a state of mind, it is a fact of life.

Muhammad Ali
(Athlete and Human Rights Activist)

I am America. I am the part you won't recognize. But get
used to me. Black, confident, cocky; my name, not yours;
my religion, not yours; my goals; my own; get use to me.

Rev. Jesse Jackson, Sr.
(Civil and Human Rights Activist)

Down with dope, up with hope

August Wilson
(Dramatist/Writer)

Freedom is heavy. You got to put your shoulder into it
and hope your back holds up.

40

As long as the colored man look to white folk to put the crown on what he say, as long as he looks to white folks for approval…then he ain't never gonna find out who he is and what he's about.

Dorothy Height
(Civil Rights Leader)

Greatness is not measured by what a man or woman accomplishes but the opposition he or she has to overcome to reach his or her goals.

Colin Powell
(Retired General, U. S. Army and first Black U.S. Secretary State)

People will say "You're a terrific black general". I'm trying to be the best general I can be.

Eldridge Cleaver
(Writer/Activist)

You're either part of the solution or part of the problem.

Mary McLeod Bethune
(Education/Civil Rights Leader)

If we accept and acquiesce in the face of discrimination,
we accept the responsibility ourselves and allow those
responsible to solve their conscience by believing that
they have our acceptance and concurrence. We should
protest openly everything…that smacks of
discrimination…

Mrs. Mamie Bradley
(Mother of Emmett Louis Till)

He didn't do anything to deserve that. Somebody is
going to pay for this. All I want to do is get my boy's
body back and give him a decent burial. Then I'll have to
go to work on this thing.

Asa Philip Randolph
(Labor and Civil Rights Leader)

We will need to continue our demonstration…return to
our communities to build fires under the Congressman.
Legislation is enacted under pressure. There has got to be
pressure.

Rev. Adam Clayton Powell, Jr.
(Former Pastor of Abyssinian Baptist Church and U. S. Congressman)

Never let blackness be your problem, but somebody else's problem.

Ronald E. McNair, Ph. D.
(Late Astronaut/Scientist)

My wish is that we would allow this planet to be the beautiful oasis that she is, and allow ourselves to live more in the peace that she generates.

Jay-Z
(Rap Artist/Entrepreneur)

The most amazing feeling I feel/Words can't describe the feeling, for real/Baby, I paint the sky blue/my greatest creation was you, you. Glory!

Harriet Tubman
(Abolitionist)

I freed a thousand slaves. I could have freed a thousand more if only they knew they were slaves.

Leontyne Price
(Opera Diva)

If you are going to think black, think positive about it. Don't think down on it, or think it is something in your way. And this way, when you really do want to stretch out and express how beautiful black is, everybody will hear you.

Malcolm X
(Former National Spokesman of Nation of Islam)

I'm for truth, no matter who tells it. I'm for justice, no matter who it's for or against.

There is nothing better than adversity. Every defeat, every heartbreak, every loss, contains its own seed, its own lesson on how to improve your performance the next time.

Booker T. Washington
(Educator/Founder of Tuskegee University)

Success is to be measured not so much by the position that one has reached in life as by the obstacles which he has overcome.

Oprah Winfrey
(Actor/Entrepreneur)

Doing the best at this moment puts you in the best place for the next moment.

As you become more clear about who you really are, you're better able to decide what is best for you, the first time around.

Do the one thing you cannot do. Fail at it. Try again. Do better the second time. The only people who never tumble are those who never mount the high wire. This is your moment. Own it.

Hank Aaron
(Hall of Fame Baseball Player and Home Run Hitter)

I never doubted my ability, but when you hear all your life you're inferior, it makes you wonder if the other guys have something you've never seen before. If they do, I'm still looking for it.

William "Bill" Cosby, Ed. D.
(Actor/Comedian)

I don't know the key to success, but the key to failure is trying to please everybody.

Even though your kids will do the exact opposite of what you're telling them to do, you have to keep loving them just as much.

Ralph Ellison
(Novelist)

I am not ashamed of my grandparents for having been slaves. I am only ashamed of myself for having at one time being ashamed.

Michael Jordan
(Hall of Fame Basketball Player/Entrepreneur)

No matter how good you are, always keep working on your game.

Oprah Winfrey
(Actor/Entrepreneur)

I still have my feet on the ground, I just wear better shoes.

Cornel West, Ph. D.
(Scholar/Activist)

Black people have always been America's wilderness in search of a promised land.

Jesse Owens
(Olympian Gold Medalist)

The battles that count aren't the ones for gold metals. The struggles within yourself-the invisible, inevitable battles inside all of us-that's where it's at.

Marvin Gaye
(Composer/Singer)

Brother, brother, there is too many of us dying. Don't speak to me of brutality. Only love can conquer hate. What's going on?

Fannie Lou Hamer
(Civil Rights Activist)

Whether you have a Ph. D, a D.D., or no D, we're in this together. Whether you're from Morehouse or No house, we're in this bag together.

William Clay
(Former U. S. Congressman)

Politically, we have no permanent friends, just permanent interest.

Rev. Jesse Jackson, Sr.
(Civil Rights Activist/Founder Rainbow Push Coalition)

Hope is the only weapon that underprivileged people have. If we give up hope, the grape will become raisin. We must stand up and fight back.

It's the Memphis agenda of Dr. King that ought to be completed…he realized that the Dream would be a nightmare, if jobs, justice, and economic opportunity was not obtained.

William "Bill" Cosby
(Actor/Comedian)

Even though your kids may not be paying attention, you have to pay attention to them all the way.

Marian Anderson
(Opera Singer)

As long as you keep a person down, some part of you has to be down there to hold him down, so it means you cannot soar as you otherwise might.

Constance Baker Motley
(Federal Judge)

I rejected the notion that my race or sex would bar my success in life.

Vernon Jordan
(Attorney/Civil Rights Activist)

I am here because I stand on many, many shoulders, and that's true of every black person I know who has achieved.

Ernest Everett Just, Ph. D.
(Biologist)

We feel the beauty of nature because we are part of nature because we know that however much in our separate domains we abstract from the unity of Nature, this unity remains. Although we may deal with particulars, we return finally to the whole pattern woven out of these…

Muhammad Ali
(Champion Boxer/Activist)

Children make you want to start life all over.

Herschel Walker
(Professional Football Star)

I keep my body in shape and it does what I tell it to do.

NAS
(Hip-Hop Artist)

I know I can

I know I can be what I wanna be if I work hard. I'll be where I wanna be,

There was empires in Africa called Kush and Timbuktu, where every race came to get books to learn from black teachers who taught Greeks and Romans, Asians, Arabs and gave them gold; when gold was converted to money it all changed. Money became empowerment for Europeans.

Slavery was money. If the truth is told the youth can grow. Nobody says you have to be gangsta, hoes. Read more learn more, change the globe

I know I can be what I wanna be

HUMOR

Dick Gregory
(Comedian)

…A strange twist in history – no one seemed to notice that the same people who resented Malcolm X put him on a stamp in 1999. When I saw the stamp, I could only say, they finally found a way to lick Malcolm.

…Last time I was down south, I walked into this restaurant. This white waitress came up to me and said we don't serve colored people here". I said, that's all right, I don't eat colored people, no way! Bring me a whole fried chicken"

Richard Pryor
(Actor/Comedian)

I went to Zimbabwe. I know how white people feel in America now; relaxed! Caused when I heard the police car I knew they weren't coming after me.

I went through every phone book in Africa, and I didn't find one goddamned Pryor.

It's been a struggle for me because I had a chance to be white and refused.

The reason people use a crucifix against vampires is that vampires are allergic to BS

I went to the White House, met the president…We in trouble. Reagan looked at me like I owed him money.

Mary the Mule
(unknown)

There once was an old man who had a wagon and a mule named Mary. This old man made his living by hauling junk. Each day he had the same routine. He would leave his house early every morning and collect junk. At noon he would stop at the bottom of the hill, eat his lunch, and feed Mary, the mule. After feeding Mary, he would start calling Mary different names (Susie, Jane, Kathy, Ernestine, Sarah Ann, etc.)

One day, two boys heard the old man talking to Mary. They started laughing at the old man. One of them said, "Old man everybody says you are crazy cause you always calling your mule all them names.   Why you do that?" The Old man said, "Well, young man, since you asked me, I'll tell you. You see that big steep hill?" "Yes, Sir," they answered. "You see all that junk in the wagon?" "Yes, Sir," the boys answered again. The old man continued, "Well boys, if I didn't make Mary think

54

she had a whole lot of help, Mary wouldn't climb that hill.'

Leroy and the Collard Greens
(Unknown)

There once was this young man who was a mathematical genius. However, he did not do well in school. His name was JT. The school officials labeled him special needs. Soon JT left school. JT's math skills became legend in the streets. JT made lots of money. JT loved his grandfather. He bought his grandfather acres of land to grow collard greens.

One day JT's math skills landed him in jail for his street banking activities. After a few weeks in jail, JT called his grandfather to see how he was doing.

JT said, "Granddaddy, how are you doing?" His granddaddy said, "Not too good since you went to jail. It is planting time and I can't get anybody to plow the land or plant the collard greens seeds. JT, I don't know what I am going to do."

JT said, "Let me think about it Granddaddy, I'll call you in a few days."

JT called his granddaddy in a few days. He said, "Just listen to me Granddaddy and don't say anything. Granddaddy, I hid all of that money on your land and a few bodies too. I will call you later in a few days."

JT called his granddaddy in a few days and said, "Granddaddy, what's happening?"

"JT, son, I'm planting seeds. The Sheriff, F.B.I. and I.R.S. all sent people out to dig up the fields. Son, they even dug up the front lawn. Boy, they sure do like you. Thank you, Son, we going to have a good crop of collard greens."

RACISM AND SOCIAL ANALYSIS

Fannie Lou Hamer
(Civil Rights Activist)

…I am sick and tired of being sick and tired…

Frances Cress Welsing, MD.
(Psychiatrist)

Contrary to Western philosophy, there are no accounts of skin-pigmented people, in their basic religious and/or philosophical texts, conceiving of themselves as being born in sin or viewing their genital apparatus card therefore their genes as the basis of sin and evil.

…in spite of the past and present potential carnage from handguns, there is a tremendous resistance amongst the dominant population to have guns as well as all other instruments of life destruction…brought under control…the gun is a critical symbol in the subconscious mind of white people everywhere. This symbol is primarily operative; as are all true symbols at the unconscious level of brain activity…increasing numbers of Black behavioral scientist are beginning to understand that the dominant thrust in what has become known as "Western civilization" is racism…

John Hope Franklin, Ph. D.
(Historian)

…increase in the size of what William Julius Wilson calls the underclass…is the remarkable demographic changes that makes it possible for today's minority – Latin Americans, Asian Americans, African Americans – to become the nation's majority within two or three decades. The possible impact of this shift on race and ethnicity is difficult to measure, but this stark fact helps explain the strident opposition by some individuals and groups to any moves that hasten the day of racial equality. The increase in the numbers and activities of groups opposed to affirmative action or other race-based remedies is the product of this phenomenon…

James Baldwin
(Author)

…the troubled American is not going to listen, does not want to know, does not want to hear the truth about the situation of the American Black"…

E. Eric Lincoln, Ph.D.
(Theologian)

…our socialization process has prepared white children to continue the privileged traditions of the established white hegemony while black children have been programmed for social and economic oblivion.

Dr. Jeremiah A. Wright, Jr.
(Theologian)

…"African American children especially need to know that this world hounds them, haunt them, and hate them because of their skin and texture of their hair…African American children have special needs in this Eurocentric wasteland and outright distortions…

Rev. C. L. Franklin
(Minister)

… honey don't say, I am not going to get in the mess. If you are born in America, with a black face, you are already in the mess.

Alvin F. Poussant, MD.
(Psychiatrist)

Many Afro-Americans expend a great deal of internal energy trying to seek individual freedom "in a white man's world. But it is a vain effort because "personal acceptability" has to be repeatedly proven to each new white group.

The Negro group's vigorous pursuit of middle-class status symbols is frequently an over determined attempt to demonstrate to the white man, as well as to themselves that they can be successful, worthwhile human beings.

Robert Hill, Ph.D.
(Sociologist)

…the persistence of many popular misconceptions about the actual nature and extent of black progress strongly suggest that such terms as "structural employment" and "underclass" may become code words for "unsolvable" and "intractable" to justify governmental inaction on behalf of racial minorities…

James P. Comer, MD.
(Psychiatrist/Educator)

The Negro experience has been very different. The
traumatic effects of separation from Africa, slavery, and
denial of political and economic opportunities after the
abolition of slavery created divisive psychological and
social forces in the Negro community.

L. L. Cool J
(Rap Artist/Actor)

Can't a young man make money anymore?

Or is it your job to be sure I'm poor?

Get the flashlight out of my face I'm not a dog so damn it
put away the mace. I got cash and real attorneys on the
case. You're joker perpetuating the ace. You got time?
You want to give me a taste? I don't smoke cigarettes so
why you lookin' for base?

Bishop Henry McNeal Turner
(Noted Abolitionist/AME Churchman)

"There is no manhood future in the United States for the Negro. He may eke out an existence for generations to come, but he can never be a man-full, symmetrical and un-dwarfed

Judge A. Leon Higginbotham, Jr.
(Federal Judge/Legal Scholar)

..."the precept of inferiority did not define any specific right or obligation. Instead "inferiority" spoke to the state of the mind and the logic of the heart..."inferiority" did not owe its existence to the legal process. When the Thirteenth Amendment abolished slavery...it did not eliminate the precept of inferiority...when the law abolished state-enforced racial segregation, it still did not eliminate the precept...

Ralph Bunche, Ph. D.
(Diplomat/Nobel Peace Prize Winner)

..."it is painfully obvious that black communities can never be economically viable except on an intolerable low standard of living...therefore, the black American under partial separation, will continue to have his economic life in the white sector. The practical result of this in time will be an American version of apartheid.

…when any black men are rejected by the dominant white society, all are rejected…There is a decisive difference between being accepted genuinely, as an equal, and being tolerated for some reason, such as recognition of ability and need for it… I am not better, nor am I angry. I rely on reason, candor, and truth…I am convinced that on the problem of race most Americans hide the truth or, more accurately, hide from it…

…This is my country. I own a share in it. I have a vested interest in it. My ancestors helped to create it, to build it, to make it strong and great and rich. All of this belongs to me as much as it belongs to any American with a white skin. What is mine I intend to have and to hold, to fight, if necessary to hold it. I will not give up my legacy in this society willingly…

Roy Wilkins
(Civil Rights Leader/former NAACP Executive)

At first color doesn't mean very much to little children, black or white. Only as they grow older and absorb poisons from adults, does color begin to blind them.

K R S – One
(Rap Artist)

It seems that when you walk the ghetto you walk with your own point of view; you judge a man by the car he drives or if his hat matches his shoes. But back in the days of Sherlock Holmes, a man was judged by a clue, now he is judged by if he's Spanish, Black, or Jew. So do not kick my door down and tie me up while my wife cooks the stew.

William Julius Wilson, Ph.D.
(Sociologist)

Crime, family dissolution, welfare, and low levels of social organization are fundamentally a consequence of the disappearance of work.

The reason that the large proportion of female-headed families in the black community is a problem is not because they're headed by women but because these families are overwhelmingly impoverished.

Constance Baker Motley
(Federal Judge)

Sexism, like racism goes with us into the next century. I see class warfare as overshadowing both.

JAZZ/MUSIC

Barry Neal
(Author)

The Blues are the ideology of the field slave, the ideology
of a new "proletariat" searching for a means of judging
the world.

Jim Hendrix
(Innovative Guitarist)

We try to make our music so loose and hard-hitting that it
hits your soul hard enough to make it open. It's like
shock therapy.

Duke Ellington
(Composer/Jazz Musician)

Lovers have come and gone, but only my mistress stays,
she waits on me hand and foot. She has grace. She is as
modern as tomorrow. Music is my mistress, and she
plays second fiddle to no one.

James Brown
(Musician/ Entertainer)

Say it loud, I'm black and I'm proud!

Art Farmer
(Jazz Musician)

Charlie Parker brought the rhythm; the way he played those notes. He was very strong intellectually and had a very strong personality.

Dizzy Gillespie
(Jazz Innovator)

Charlie Parker...the method and music impressed me, the more I heard him play. His style was perfect for our music. You know, he used to do tunes inside of times. He was the most fantastic musician.

It's very sad that this music is put on the side, and not many people know about the importance of this art form we call jazz. And the other sad thing is whenever someone has to educate people in film about this art form they always miss the mark. They never show the brilliance of improvisation and what it really is.

There is a parallel with jazz and religion. In jazz a messenger comes to the music and spreads his influence to a critical point, and then another comes and takes you further. In religion – in the spiritual sense – God picks certain individuals from this world to lead mankind up to a certain point of spiritual development.

Jazz is beautiful. It brings beauty and deeper values to people's lives, so they can touch the deeper parts inside themselves. If the leaders of the world bring this music to the people of the world there would be a different mentality.

Monk and I began to work out some complex variations on chords, and we'd use them at night to scare away no – talent guys. After a while, we got interested in what we were doing as music, and we began to explore more and more, our music evolved.

Miles Davis
(Jazz Innovator)

You have to pay for fame…mentally, spiritually, and in real money.

After you make all this music, please all these people with your playing, and are known all over the world, you find out all it takes is a commercial to put you over the top in people's minds. All you've got to do in this country today is just be on television and you are more known and respected than anyone who paints a great painting or creates great music or writes a great book.

Black people are acting out roles every day in this country just to keep on getting by…they put on masks and do great acting jobs just to get through the…day.

…not long after Trane and I were playing together…I use to pinch myself to see if I was really there…Trane was a diamond himself, and I knew it, and everybody else who heard him knew it, too.

Kind of Blue came from church gospel. I started remembering what that music sounded like and felt like. I wrote this blues…I tried to get back that feeling…that I was trying to get close to.

I learned a lot from Bird…picking up from the way he played or didn't play a musical phrase or idea. His creativity and musical ideas were endless. He could play so many different styles and never repeat the same musical idea.

There was a hip -ness in black people then…they were serious about their partying and listening to music. People were really listening to what you were playing. If you weren't playing anything, they would let you know.

Thelonious Monk's use of space in his solos and his manipulation of funny – sounding chord progressions just knocked me out…Monk's use of space had a big influence on the way I played solos…

Jazz is about style.

Music is always changing. It changes because of the times, the technology that's available; the materials that things are made of…musicians pick up sounds and incorporate that into their playing…

As far as where my music is going, I'm always trying to hear something new.

Bebop was about change, about evolution. It wasn't about standing still and becoming safe. If anybody wants to keep creating they have to be about change.

Thelonious Monk
(Jazz Innovator)

Every sound influenced Diz. He had that kind of mind, you know? And he influenced everything too.

A note can be as small as a pin or as big as the world, it depends on your imagination.

If you really understand the meaning of bebop, you understand the meaning of freedom.

Hubert Walter
(Musicologist)

…"we must realize the over-whelming affect of the black music idiom is real, and its affect on American music is overpowering. Black musicians are providing the impetus for one of the most radical transition of musical styles in the whole of music…"

Wynton Marsalis
(Jazz Musician)

The blues is a down home sound. It makes you feel good, like you're down home, which is always where you want to be.

You know I felt all the whole disappointment of all the people in my family…I could feel all that. And it was profound, and it was real. That's where the jazz musician would be coming from to me. You know soul.

…Coltrane is the towering figure… he understood that compassion means having a commitment to something bigger than he himself…

…"Jazz music was invented to let us know how to listen to each other, how to negotiate…you've to listen to people.   Because, if you aren't listening to them, you can't play with them.

Lee Morgan
(Jazz Trumpeter)

There are no natural barriers. It's either hip or it ain't.

Jackie McLean
(Educator/Jazz Saxophonist)

I tell my students, "It's an important tradition and you have to go back and hear this music and learn its language all the way through. How you going to know what's new to play, if you haven't listened to everything that's old?"

Louis Satchmo Armstrong
(Jazz Trumpeter/Innovator)

My whole life, my whole soul, is to blow that horn. What we play is life.

All music is folk music. I ain't never heard no horse sing a song.

Man, if you have to ask what it (jazz) is, you'll never know.

Howlin Wolf
(Blues Musician)

I put a spell on you, cause you're mine.

RELIGION

Dr. Martin L. King, Jr.

Love is the most durable power in the world. This creative force, so beautifully exemplified in the life of our Christ, is the most potent instrument available in mankind's quest for peace and security.

The belief that God will do everything for man is as untenable as the belief that man can do everything for himself. It, too, is based on a lack of faith. We must learn that to expect God to do everything while we do nothing is not faith but superstition.

Science investigates; religion interprets. Science gives man knowledge which is power; religion gives man wisdom which is control. They are complimentary.

Rev. Farrell Duncombe
(Past Grand Chaplain Omega Psi Phi Fraternity, Inc.)

Life's greatest wars are fought on the battlefield of the mind. Life's most serious conflict is inner conflict, and the scars of war that inflict the most permanent wound and cause the greatest pain are to be found not on the skin, but on the soul.

John P. Kee
(Pastor/Gospel Musician)

His word is sweeter than the sweetest honeycomb.

Dr. Samuel D. Proctor
(Theologian)

With all of our technological achievement and major advancements in medicine, here we are no better off morally and spiritually than those people a long time ago who first heard Jesus tell about a man who fell among thieves on the Jericho road. We have to recognize the lack of compassion of our cities, our government, our communities…we gotten so use to it that we're practically numb to inhumanity, to the callous indifference that surrounds us. We need to recover a sense of human compassion.

One of the most searching questions that every life must ask is whether or not this world is a friendly place. If one does not find an operative, coherent answer to that question the alienation and estrangement that follow can be pathological. Early in life, at the threshold of reason, one must be exposed to an interpretation of the world that is satisfactory to the mind and soul…

Everybody is God's somebody. This in the main lesson that we must get across to many black youth today...we must convince them that no matter how the society perceives them or treats them...they are loved with an infinite love.

After slaves fought for their freedom and the abolition of slavery was accomplished in 1865, some of them were free on the books but not free in their minds and hearts. Some others were free in mind, free in spirit, and free in heart long before they were free on the books...they took flight and left their old identities behind...The freedom that Christ gives us is impelled by his Spirit...

Kenneth L. Walters, Sr.
(Theologian)

Where do we get this idea...that just because God is Spirit that God's is colorless? Where does the idea of the colorless, shapeless, featureless God come from? Why would God, who made the colors and called them good, deny God self of color? Yes, God is invisible to us, but must that mean that God is a formless, characterless, colorless heavenly haze...when God revealed God self to Ezekiel and to John...God was revealed as a person of dark color...

The chief point is that if God could use black people in such great ways in the past, God can still use us in great ways today. I know that this hard for some of us to believe. We do not feel like instruments of anything constructive. We feel useless and hopeless. But in the midst of the hopelessness and oppression, we have a word, we have a word from the Lord saying, "Our day is coming".

Dr. Henry H. Mitchell
(Theologian)

God exercises the right to squeeze a blessing out of even the worst of injustices, after we have done all we can to remove them.

Dr. Evan E. Crawford
(Dean Emeritus Andrew Rankin Memorial Chapel, Howard University)

It's not the tool that makes you free; it's the truth that makes you free.

Dr. Jeremiah Wright
(Theologian)

In our day and age, some black people call God "Allah" and say As salaam alaikum. In our day and age, some black people call God "Yahweh" and say "Shalom alechem". In our day and age, some black people call God "Ra" and Ammon Ra' and they greet each new day saying "Hotep"…I call him "Bread" when I'm hungry and "Water" when I'm thirsty…I am sticking with our tradition…

Imam W. Deen Mohammed
(Spiritual Leader American Muslim Mission)

Sensationalism and consumerism enslave the human spirit…Traditional human pride suffers a sell out on hood blocks…not slave blocks anymore, they are hood blocks, because anything that takes your human values out of you and takes your human spirit…that thing enslaves you…

We cannot manage this creation by ourselves…care about yourself enough to protect yourself…if you let your morals be changed, if you let the way you see right and wrong be changed, you are letting a killer kill you. The killer is the bad influence in…society. Fight these things'.

Rev. Dr. Bernard Jakes
(Pastor)

Do not allow your physical vision to overcome your mental vision or you will become a permanent victim.

Dr. Howard Thurman
(Pioneering Theologian)

…"the human spirit is capable of great nobility"…

…"I make a careful distinction between Christianity and the religion of Jesus. My judgment about slavery and racial prejudice relative to Christianity is far more devastating than yours…"

The name marks the claim a man stakes against the world…it is his announcement to life that he is present and accounted for in all his parts…to be known, to be called by one's name is to find one's place and hold it against all the hordes of hell…

Adam C. Powell, Jr.
(Politician/Preacher)

I am the product of the sustained indignation of a
branded grandfather, the militant protest of my
grandmother, the disciplined resentment of my father
and mother, and the power of the mass action of the
church.

Marcus Garvey
(Founder Negro Improvement Association)

...There is no fear, but the fear of God. Man cannot drive
fear into the heart of man because man is but the equal of
man...

Minister Louis Farrakhan
(National Minister, Nation of Islam)

You've got the Name of Jesus, but you don't have the
Spirit of Jesus, if you had his Spirit the work would be
done. The evil scientists who are ruling society have set
up a world contrary to God's will. They make evil seem
good. They promote filth and indecency, as well as
unhealthy foods that have an easily observable negative
effect on the body.

Bishop T. D. Jakes
(Author/Theologian)

God plants an infinitely curious mind within every little child and adolescent. As they grow older, many children bend to indifference and ignorance, while others surrender to scorn and punishment, and eventually most will finally succumb to a "formal education" that will quench their natural hunger for knowledge.

Within every man dwells the little child who preceded him. Manhood is rooted in childhood and many of the thoughts you and I have today come from our early experiences as children.

Man was created to dwell in God's presence...We feel after Him like blind men groping in the dark. We push towards him like searching thirsty roots penetrate dry ground...

You can be surrounded by people and still be alone if God is after you...Who are you when all the camouflage is off...?

Anybody can assign his agenda to you if you don't know who you are. Unless you confront your own frailties and map your own vulnerabilities, you will never be prepared for attacks in those areas.

Sojourner Truth
(Abolitionist)

Religion without humanity is very poor human stuff.

James Weldon Johnson
(Author, Composer, Diplomat, Civil Rights Leader)

Lift every voice and sing, until earth and heaven ring.

Young man, young man, your arm is too short to box
with God.

John Coltrane
(Composer/musician)

A Love Supreme. Have no fear…blessed be his name.
One thought can produce millions of vibrations and they
all go back to God…everything does. His way… it is so
lovely …A love Supreme.

Bishop Richard Allen
(First Bishop African Methodist Episcopal Church)

The Lord was pleased to strengthen us, and remove all fear from us, and disposed our hearts to be useful as possible.

Charles W. Chestnut
(Author)

Sins, like chickens, come home to roost.

Dr. Chancellor Williams
(Historian)

...the future task before Black Muslim and Black Christians is distinguishing their true religion from how evil men have used it to serve their own non-religious purposes...

Frederick Douglas

One and God makes a majority.

Marian Anderson
(Opera Singer)

Prayers begin where human capacity ends.

Satchel Paige
(Pioneering Athlete)

Don't pray when it rains if you don't pray when the sun shines.

Pearl Bailey
(Actress/Singer)

People see God every day, they just don't recognize Him.

George Washington Carver
(Scientist)

Our creator is the same and never changes despite the name given Him by people here and in all parts of the world. Even if we gave Him no name at all, He would still be there within us, waiting to give us good on this earth.

Dr. Gardner C. Taylor
(Dean of Black Preachers)

We need faith in the future in order for life to be sweet as we grow older.

Dull days may dawn; dark clouds may hover, but press on!!

Keep your eyes open for sin shows itself for what it is. It is a hair fooling us. A murderer killing us and a troublemaker confusing us.

Sad are the people who tried to meet tough times in their own power.

For we do not know who we are because we do not know whose we are. We have lost the awareness that we are children of God.

I believe love inevitably invariably involves vulnerability: you cannot love and be invulnerable.

Stop saying, I am lucky. No idle luck sits at the heart of the universe, but God is in command of all things.

Hope will keep us marching when strength is gone. Hope speaks to souls when we are loss.

COLLOQUIALISMS AND SONG

I am down with it and just can't quit it.
(Unknown)

Blues Lyrics

You take it like you find it and you leave it like it is. That
is the way love is, that is the way it's going to be.

John O. Killens
(Novelist)

Ain't no more Mississippi

Ain't no more Mississippi

It's jes' Sippi from now on?

I am loose as a goose and I'm out here.
(Unknown)

What you know about this youngblood? You better listen.
(Unknown)

Be cool, baby. Don't be no fool.
(Unknown)

Let me pull your coat, Jack.
(Unknown)

Drop it like its hot.
(Unknown)

He was so cool, he froze.
(Unknown)

Stop looking sad in the face as a mule pulling a hearse.
(Unknown)

Wait? I'm not waiting on Nothing. Wait, broke the
wagon.
(Unknown)

The blacker the berry, the sweeter the juice
(Unknown)

Look at what you get when you lucky and don't want
what you got.
(Unknown)

Look out now!
(Unknown)

Word up!
(Unknown)

Let the door hit you where God split you.
(Unknown)

It's your world. If I had your hand I'd give mine up.
(Unknown)

Curtis Mayfield
(Composer/Musician)

Keep on pushing and maybe someday I'll reach that
higher goal.

Tell it like it T'IS......
(Unknown)

Don't be no square.
(Unknown)

I have been blessed by the best.
(Unknown)

Preston Foster
(Blues Composer/Musician)

I got my MOJO working, but it just won't work on you. I
want to love you
I got my black cat bones all pure and dry
I got my four leaf clovers all hanging high
I got my hoodoo ashes, but it just won't work on you.

Last Poets
(Musicians)

The revolution will not be televised.

Free your mind and your behind will follow.
(Unknown)

Everything is everything.
(Unknown)

Keep the faith, baby.
(Unknown)

Keep it on wood and it will always be good.
(Unknown)

Stop dipping in the kool-aid without
knowing the flavor.
(Unknown)

Get down with it!
(Unknown)

Go head with your badd-self.
(Unknown)

Keep it in sight and it won't be no fight.
(Unknown)

Sock it to them.
(Unknown)

A black snake will kill you, just as quick as a white snake.
(Unknown)

Hit me with the 411.
(Unknown)

Don't play me!
(Unknown)

You better be yourself, before you be by yourself.
(Unknown)

I ain't giving up nothing but bubble gum and potato chips. And, I am fresh out of both .So you know what I'm giving up.
(Unknown)

Ought from ought, leaves ought.
(Unknown)

EPILOGUE

Dr. Benjamin E. Mays
(Educator/Theologian)

Life is just a minute only sixty seconds in it, forced upon you can't refuse it. Didn't seek it, didn't choose it, but it's up to you to use it. You must suffer if you lose it, give an account if you abuse it just a tiny little minute, but eternity is in it.

Aime Cesaire
(Poet)

The race of man is only just beginning, and there is room for all of us at the rendezvous of history.

SOURCES

Akbar, Na'im.   From Mis-education to Education.
Jersey City, NJ: New Mind Productions 1982

Alexander E. Curtis.   Elijah Muhammad on African
American Education New York. Chesapeake: ECA
Associates 1989

Anderson, Claude.   Black Labor: White Wealth,
Edgewood, MD: Duncan & Duncan, Inc. Publisher 1994

Barbour, Floyd B. (Editor).   The Black Power Revolt: A
collection of Essays. New York: Collier Books 1971

Bennett, Jr., Jerome.   Before the Mayflower: A History
of Black America.
Chicago: Johnson Publishing Co., Inc. 2003

Clarke, John Henrik (ed).   Marcus Garvey and the
Vision of Africa. New York: Vantage Books – Random
House 1974

Colston, Freddie C.   Dr. Benjamin E. May Speaks
Lanham, Maryland: University Press of America, Inc.
2002

Copiage, Eric V. Black Pearls for Parents. New York:
William Morrow 1995

Crew, Rudy and Dyja, Thomas.   Only Connect: The Way to Save our Schools. New York: Sarah Crichton Books 2007

Davis, Miles and Troupe, Quincy. Miles: The Autobiography. New York: Simon and Schuster, Inc. 1989 University Press 1998

Foster, Benjamin. Looking For Payoff: A New Schooling For African-American Inner-City Youth. Jersey City, NJ: New Mind Productions, Inc. 1990

Franklin, John Hope and Moss, Jr., Alfred A.   From Slavery to Freedom.   Boston: McGraw-Hill 2000

Gregory, Dick and Moses, Sheila P. Callus on My Soul. New York: Kensington Publishing Corporation 2000

Hale, Janice E. Black Children: Their Roots, Culture, and Learning Styles. Baltimore: John Hopkins University Press 1982

Hrabowski, Freeman. A, III, Maton Kenneth I., and Greif, Geoffrey L. Beating the Odds: Raising Academically Successful African American Males. New York: Oxford University Press 1998

Higginbotham, Jr., A. Leon. Shades of Freedom. New York – Oxford: Oxford University Press 1996

Hilliard, Asa G. The Maroon Within Us. Baltimore: Black Classic Press 1995

Jakes, T. D. Loose That Man, Let Him Go! Tulsa, Oklahoma: Allbury Press 1995

King, Coretta Scott The Words of Martin Luther King, Jr. New York: Newmarket Press 1983

Kozol, Jonathan. Savage Inequalities: Children in America Schools. New York: Crown Publishers, Inc. 1991

Lewis, Reginald and Walker, Blain S. Why Should the White Guys Have All the Fun? Baltimore: Black Classic Books 2005

Mitchell, Henry H. Celebration and Experience in Preaching. Nashville: Abingdon Press 1990

Muhammad, Elijah. Message To The Black Man. Chicago: Muhammad Temple No. 2 1963

Proctor, Samuel D. and Watley, William D., Sermons From the Black Pulpit. Valley Forge: Judson Press 1984

Rose, Tricia. Black Noise: Rap Music and Black Culture in Contemporary America. Hanover, NH: Wesleyan University Press 1994

Tanner, Lee. Dizzy: John Binks Gillespie in His 75th Year. Petaluma, California: Pomegranate Artbooks 1991

Urquhart, Brian. Ralph Bunche: An American Life New York: W. W. Norton & Company 1993

Thurman, Howard With Head and Heart. San Diego: Harcourt Brace and Company 1979

_____ The Inward Journey. Richmond, Indiana: Friends United Press 1961

Waters, Kenneth. Afrocentric Sermons: The Beauty of Blackness in the Bible. Valley Forge: Judson Press 1993

Weinberg, Meyer (editor) WEB DuBois: A Reader. New York: Harper and Row Publishers 1970

Welsing, Frances Cress. The Isis Papers: The Keys To The Colors. Chicago: Third World Press 1991

West, Cornel. Restore Hope. Boston: Beacon Press 1997

Woodson, Carter, G. The Mis-Education of the Negro. Trenton, NJ: African World Press, Inc. 1990

Wright, Nathan, Jr. (editor) What Black Educators are Saying. New York: Hawthorn Books, Inc. 1970

Williams, Chancellor. The Destruction of Black Civilization: Great Issues of A Race From 4500 B.C. 20 2000 A.D. Chicago: Third World Press 1987

Yette, Samuel E. <u>The Choice: The issue of Black Survival in America.</u> New York: Berkley Publishing Corp 1971

PERIODICAL REFERENCES

The Black Scholar Journal of Black Studies and Research vol. 10 no. 2 October 1978

Op cit vol. 7 no. 3 November 1975

Op cit vol. 3 no. 10 Summer 1972

Op cit May – June 1973

Op cit vol. 3. No. 3 November 1971

Marshall, Thurgood *The Oral Argument Before the Supreme Court* in <u>Brown vs. Board of Education</u> Topeka. 1952 – 1955

Life: The Final Battlefield-Part I by Wath D. Muhammad Muslim Journal vol. 38, No. 23 March 1, 2013 pg. 15

The African American Pulpit vol. 5 no. 2 Spring 2002

Op cit vol. 5 no. 3 Summer 2002

Op cit vol. 6 no. 1 Winter 2002-2003

Imam W. Deen Mohammed Speaks to "Stop The Violence" Rally In Philadelphia, Pennsylvania vol. 38, no. 32, May 3, 2013

The Muslim Journal

The Washington Afro American vol. 122 no. 4 September
6, 2013

ABOUT THE AUTHOR

Dr. Benjamin Foster, Jr. is a public intellectual and former public school administrator, serving in several positions in Connecticut, New York City, and North Carolina. He served as the first African American Principal Planning Analyst for Human Services, Connecticut State Office of Policy and Management and Assistant Chief, Staff Development, Department of Social Services. He has lectured in several colleges.

He is the author of **Looking for Payoff: A New Schooling for African American Inner-City Youth**, in which he explored the dropout problem. In addition, he has published several articles on the social condition of African Americans including the highly cited "The Case for Vouchers" which appeared in the **Black Scholar**. Dr. Foster earned a Bachelor's degree in Sociology from Trinity College, a Master's in History degree from Wesleyan University, a Certificate of Advanced

Graduate Study and Doctoral degree in Education Administration from the University of Massachusetts/Amherst, and Certificate of Education Public Policy, George Washington University; and Certificate of Higher Education Leadership, Hampton University.

Dr. Foster is the recipient of several civic and professional awards and fellowships including: National Urban Fellow; Institute for Education Leadership Public Policy Program; Education Finance Fellow, Harvard Center for the Study of Public Policy; The Environment and Behavior Research Center, University of Massachusetts/Amherst; Administrator of the Year; Trinity College Person of the Year; and, Omega Psi Phi Fraternity, Inc., District Man of the year. He has received citations from New York African Studies Association, Hartford Chapter National Association of Negro Business and Professional Women, Delta Sigma Theta Sorority, Inc., Urban League and NAACP.

Dr. Foster's civic involvement has included the Conference churches; Biblical Institute for Social Change; Delegate New England Board of Higher Education; Trustee, Trinity College in Hartford; Board of directors, Connecticut Association of Adult and Continuing Education. He is a member of Omega Psi Phi and Sigma Pi Phi Fraternities.

He is married and has two sons.